VOLUME 4

Solos for Young Violists

Compiled and Edited by Violist **Barbara Barber**

Viola by Christian Pederson, Albuquerque, 2002
From the collection of Robertson & Sons Violin Shop, Inc., Albuquerque, NM
Photo by Justin Robertson

© 2004 Summy-Birchard Music
a division of Summy-Birchard, Inc.
Exclusive print rights administered by Alfred Music Publishing Co., Inc.
All Rights Reserved. Printed in USA.

ISBN 1-58951-187-5

INTRODUCTION

Solos for Young Violists is a five-volume series of music books with companion CDs featuring 34 works for viola and piano. Many of the pieces in this collection have long been recognized as stepping stones to the major viola repertoire, while others are newly discovered, arranged and published for this series; most are premier recordings. Compiled, edited and recorded by violist Barbara Barber, *Solos for Young Violists* is a graded series of works ranging from elementary to advanced levels and represents an exciting variety of styles and techniques for violists. The collection has become a valuable resource for teachers and students of all ages. The piano track recorded on the second half of each CD gives the violist the opportunity to practice with accompaniments.

Contents

Album Leaves
Op. 39
I.

Hans Sitt
1850-1922

II.

9

III.

IV.

V.

Tempo I

VI.

Pastorale and Gavotte

Op. 32, No. 1

Hermann Ritter
1849-1926

Gavotte ♩ = 76

Six Studies in English Folksong
I.
Lovely on the Water

R. Vaughan Williams
1872-1958

II.
Spurn Point

III.
Young Henry the Poacher

IV.
She Borrowed Some of Her Mother's Gold

V.
The Pride of Kildare

VI.
As I Walked Over London Bridge

Allegro vivace ♩ = 144

for Bernard Shore

Air and Dance

Gordon Jacob
1895-1984